Play With Me

by Barrie Wade and Hannah Wood

Play with me.

Play with me.

Play with me.

Play with me.

Play with me.

Play with me.

Play with me.

Play with me.

Story trail

Start at the beginning of the story trail. Ask your child to retell the story in their own words, pointing to each picture in turn to recall the sequence of events.

Independent Reading

This series is designed to provide an opportunity for your child to read on their own. These notes are written for you to help your child choose a book and to read it independently.

In school, your child's teacher will often be using reading books which have been banded to support the process of learning to read. Use the book band colour your child is reading in school to help you make a good choice. *Play With Me* is a good choice for children reading at Pink 1a in their classroom to read independently.

The aim of independent reading is to read this book with ease, so that your child enjoys the story and relates it to their own experiences.

About the book
Everybody is too busy to play with the little girl in this story and she is getting fed up. Luckily, the family dog is always ready to play.

Before reading
Help your child to learn how to make good choices by asking: "Why did you choose this book? Why do you think you will enjoy it?" Look at the cover together and ask: "What do you think the story will be about?" Support your child to think about what happens when they can't find anyone to play with. "What do you play when you are playing on your own?" Read the title aloud and ask: "Why might the little girl want someone to play with?" Remind your child that they can try to sound out the letters to make a word if they get stuck. Decide together whether your child will read the story independently or read it aloud to you. When books are short, as at Pink 1a, your child may wish to do both!

During reading

If reading aloud, support your child if they hesitate or ask for help by telling the word. Remind your child of what they know and what they can do independently.

If reading to themselves, remind your child that they can come and ask for your help if stuck.

After reading:

Support understanding of the story by asking your child to tell you what the story is about.

Help your child think about the messages in the book that go beyond the story and ask: "Do you think the little girl looks different on the last page? Do you think she could have played with the ball on her own? Why/why not?"

Give your child a chance to respond to the story: "Did you have a favourite part? What would you do if everybody was too busy to play with you?"

Use the story trail to encourage your child to retell the story in the right sequence, in their own words.

Extending learning

Help your child understand the story structure by using the same sentence structure with a different verb to make a new story. A child who wants to play hide and seek (Hide with me) or a child who is on a trampoline or bouncy castle (Jump with me), for example.

Your child's teacher will be encouraging accurate finger pointing at Pink 1a. Help your child learn to recognise and find commonly used words. Ask them to point to each of the words in turn on each page, starting with *play* and then *me* as these words are the easiest to find.

Franklin Watts
First published in Great Britain in 2017
by The Watts Publishing Group

Copyright © The Watts Publishing Group 2017

Series Editors: Jackie Hamley and Melanie Palmer
Series Advisors: Dr Sue Bodman and Glen Franklin
Series Designer: Peter Scoulding

A CIP catalogue record for this book is
available from the British Library.

ISBN 978 1 4451 5405 3 (hbk)
ISBN 978 1 4451 5406 0 (pbk)

Printed in China

Franklin Watts
An imprint of
Hachette Children's Group
Part of The Watts Publishing Group
Carmelite House
50 Victoria Embankment
London EC4Y 0DZ

An Hachette UK Company
www.hachette.co.uk

www.franklinwatts.co.uk